ELC

SCIENCE AND YOUR BODY

Rebecca Heddle

Designed by Sue Grobecker
Illustrated by Kate Davies
Consultant: Mary Dodge

Contents

About your body

Lots of different parts inside your body work together to keep you alive. This book will help you find out more about your body. The first experiments are about skin.

Mending skin

When you hurt your skin, your body mends it. Your blood makes a scab to cover the place until new skin is ready.

Stretchy skin

Look at your hand. You can see how well your skin fits. It is creased where it needs to fold, and when you spread out your hand, it stretches.

Draw a caterpillar on the inside of your elbow with face paints.

Bend and stretch your arm. The caterpillar shrinks and stretches with your skin.

Cooling down

You sweat when you are hot. Sweat is salty water that comes out of tiny holes in your skin. Try this to see what sweat is for.

Pour some water on the back of one hand. Keep the other one dry.

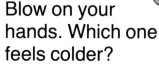

Blow on your hands. Which one feels colder?

The water cools you as it dries. Sweat cools you in the same way.

Fingerprinting

Your skin is different from other people's. Here is a way to prove this.

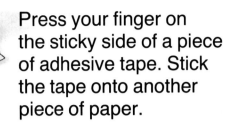

Press your finger on the sticky side of a piece of adhesive tape. Stick the tape onto another piece of paper.

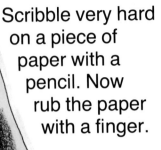

Scribble very hard on a piece of paper with a pencil. Now rub the paper with a finger.

Keep your finger flat.

You have made a print that shows the pattern of the skin on your finger.

Make prints with your other fingers. They may make different patterns. Ask some friends to make fingerprints in the same way.

Prints for proof

The police keep a copy of criminals' fingerprints. They check if these prints appear at the scene of a crime, to prove who was involved.

Look closely at the fingerprints. No one else's will be quite like yours, unless you have a twin. Then your fingerprints may match.

Me

Oliver

Leo

3

Touch

You feel things outside you with your skin. This is called your sense of touch. It tells you whether things are warm, cold, soft, hard, or scratchy.

Feeling things

You need different things of the same shape and size for this test. Here are some you could try.

Bread roll

Tennis ball

Orange

Apple

Peach

Tickling test

Try tickling a friend gently in different places. Try his hands, feet, back, and elbows. Does it tickle as much in every place?

Ask a friend to blindfold you, and put the things in front of you. Can you tell them apart with your elbow? Now try with a foot, and then with a hand.

It is hard to feel differences between things with your elbows.

Most people's feet are very ticklish, but not very good at telling things apart.

Your skin is more ticklish in some places than others. Ticklish places can feel light touches very easily.

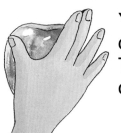

Your hands can feel small differences between things. They are a very sensitive part of your body.

4

Cold touch

Hold one hand in a bowl of ice cubes. Count to 30. Now dry your hand and try to pick up some grains of rice.

It is hard to pick up the rice because your sense of touch does not work as well when your skin is cold.

Reading hands

Braille is a sort of printing, made of patterns of raised dots on thick paper. Blind people read it with their hands. They read by recognizing the different patterns.

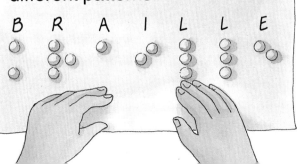

Fool your senses

Fill three big bowls with water – one hot, one cold and one warm. Put the warm one in the middle.

Put one hand in the cold bowl and one in the hot. Count to 30. Now move both hands to the middle bowl. Does the water feel hot or cold?

The warm water is hotter than the cold water. It feels hot to the hand that came from the cold bowl.

The same water feels cold to your other hand, because it is colder than the water in the hot bowl. Your sense of touch only tells you how the water in the middle bowl feels different to each hand.

5

Looking out

Your eyes need light for you to see. Try these experiments to find out more about how you see.

Light and dark

Take some crayons into an unlit room at night. You can see a little after a while, because there is always some light.

Look at the crayons. How easy is it to tell them apart?

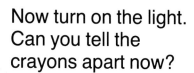

Now turn on the light. Can you tell the crayons apart now?

When there is only a little light you can see the shapes of things but not whether they are red, blue, green or orange. You need more light to see this too.

Seeing sideways

Look straight ahead. Ask a friend to move a pencil all the way around your head, level with your eyes. Tell him when you see it appear and disappear.

Keep your head still.

You can see things at the side of your head as well as in front of you, even if you are only looking ahead.

Seeing all around

Some animals, like mice, have eyes on the sides of their heads. They can see almost all around to keep a look-out for danger.

Two views

Each of your eyes sees a different view.

Hold up a pencil, and close one eye. Line the pencil up with something in the distance. Now swap eyes without moving the pencil.

Left eye closed

Right eye closed

The pencil seems to jump, because each of your eyes sees it from a different place.

When both of your eyes are open, your brain puts together the two views that they see. This makes one very clear picture.

Tricky pictures

You cannot always trust what you see. Here are some pictures that may confuse you. They are called optical illusions.

Which shape is bigger?

Are these red lines straight?

Use a ruler to find out if you are right.

Looking both ways

Chameleons' eyes can look in opposite directions at the same time. Nobody knows how their brains make sense of the pictures.

Speaking out

Your voice is made in your throat. It comes out through your mouth.

Feel your voice

There is a ridged lump in the front of your neck. Touch it. If you sing you can feel it moving.

There are two stretchy flaps of skin in this ridged lump. They are called your vocal cords. They wobble as air moves past them. This is called vibrating. It makes the sound of your voice.

This shows the ridged lump in your throat. It is part of the tube your breath comes through.

Vocal cords

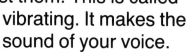

If you could see down your throat, your vocal cords would look a bit like this.

Balloon voice

Blow up a balloon. Stretch its neck tightly and let the air out. What do you hear?

The balloon squeals because the escaping air makes its stretched neck vibrate. It stops squealing as the air runs out.

Make a small cardboard tube and put it in the balloon's neck. Blow it up again. Now it does not squeal as the air escapes. The tube holds the sides of the neck still, so they cannot vibrate.

Muscles stretch your vocal cords when you speak. When your vocal cords are not stretched, they are still, so they do not make a noise.

8

Seeing vibrations

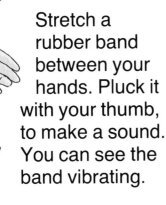

Stretch a rubber band between your hands. Pluck it with your thumb, to make a sound. You can see the band vibrating.

Try stretching the rubber band more. Can you make a different note?

Your vocal cords vibrate like rubber bands. When they are tightly stretched, they make a high note. When they are less stretched, they make a lower note.

Cricket songs

Other creatures make sounds in very different ways. Bush crickets make a singing noise by rubbing their wings together to make them vibrate.

Shaping sounds

If you want to make different sounds, you need to use your mouth as well as your vocal cords.

Sing a note. Push your lips out while you are singing, then smile broadly. You can hear the sound you are making change to "oo", and then to "ee".

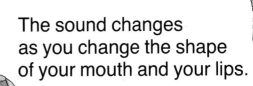

The sound changes as you change the shape of your mouth and your lips.

9

In your ears

Your ears help you hear, and they help you balance. All the working parts are hidden inside your head.

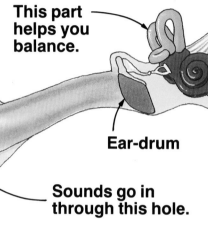

This part helps you balance.

Ear-drum

Sounds go in through this hole.

This is the only part outside your head.

Feeling sound

Hold a balloon in front of your mouth, and sing. What can you feel?

The sound of you singing travels through the air. It hits the balloon's skin and makes it wobble, or vibrate.

Your ear-drum is a stretchy part inside your ear. It vibrates when sounds hit it, like the balloon. Your brain can tell what sounds make the vibrations.

Catching sound

Hold your hands in front of your ears, like this, and talk. Still talking, move your hands behind your ears. Can you hear better now?

Hands in front of your ears stop sounds from your mouth from getting into your ears.

Hands behind your ears catch the sounds so they go into your ears. This helps you to hear your voice better.

Keeping your balance

There are tiny curved tubes in your ears with liquid inside them. Your brain can tell from the way the liquid moves how you are changing position. You can notice any sudden change and stop yourself from falling over.

The tubes look like this.

Pour some water into a bottle and move it around. The water moves as you change the bottle's position, like the liquid in your balance tubes.

Getting dizzy

Spin around ten times in a place where you won't hurt yourself if you fall over. When you stop, you feel dizzy.

To see why it happens, fill a see-through plastic bottle with water. Shake in some glitter, and put on the lid.

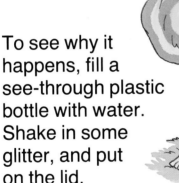

Spin the bottle, then stop it quickly. Does the glitter stop spinning too?

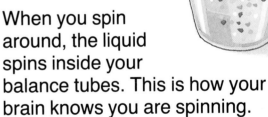

The glitter keeps spinning because the water inside the bottle keeps moving after the bottle has stopped.

When you spin around, the liquid spins inside your balance tubes. This is how your brain knows you are spinning.

You get dizzy because the liquid keeps moving after you have stopped spinning. This makes your brain think you are still spinning, so you feel dizzy.

11

Breathing

There are two big spongy bags in your chest called lungs. Each time you breathe, your lungs fill with air and empty again.

This shows where your lungs are inside you.

In and out

Lie on your back. Put one hand on your chest and one on your stomach. Breathe deeply. Can you feel your chest and stomach move?

Bones called ribs move to make your chest bigger and smaller. A muscle under your chest helps by moving up and down. It is called your diaphragm (say die-a-fram).

Breathing model

You can make air move in and out of this model.

1. Ask an adult to cut a see-through plastic bottle in half. Stretch a balloon over the neck, and push it inside.

2. Stretch a piece of a plastic bag over the open end of the bottle. Tape it all around so there are no gaps.

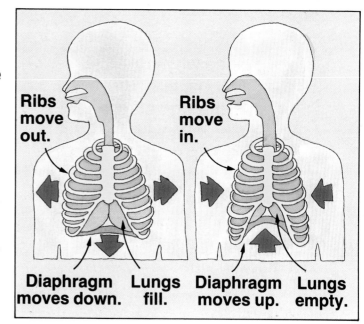

Ribs move out.

Ribs move in.

Diaphragm moves down. Lungs fill.

Diaphragm moves up. Lungs empty.

3. Tape a strip of paper to the middle of the plastic.

4. Pull down the plastic by pulling the strip, then push it up again. What happens to the balloon?

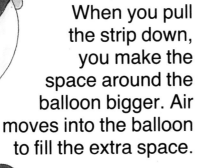

When you pull the strip down, you make the space around the balloon bigger. Air moves into the balloon to fill the extra space.

When you push it up again, you make the space smaller again, and push out the air.

Your lungs fill with air in the same way. When your chest gets bigger, air moves into your lungs. When it gets smaller, the air is pushed out again.

How much air?

Fill a see-through plastic bottle with water. Put on the lid. Hold it upside down in a bowl of water and take off the lid.

Don't let in any air.

Push a bendy straw into the neck of the bottle. Hold the bottle upright. Breathe in, then blow gently into the straw.

Don't let the straw come out.

All the air you blow out collects at the top of the bottle. You can see how much air there is in one breath.

Bones and muscles

Lots of different kinds of bones fit together inside your body. They make a framework that holds you up. It is called your skeleton.

Bending

You can bend in the places where your bones fit together. These places are called joints.

Try moving around without bending your arms and legs. Can you sit down? Can you get up again? How about scratching your head?

Now bend your arms and legs. Some joints only bend up and down. Others can move in a circle.

14

Make a model arm

You can make a model joint that bends up and down like your elbow.

Cut two strips of cardboard, one twice as wide as the other. Give the narrow strip one rounded end.

Fold the wide strip in half lengthwise. Put the rounded end of the other strip in the fold. Join them with a paper fastener.

Rounded end

Folded strip

Tape a paper hand onto the end of the folded strip of cardboard.

This model can only bend one way, like your elbow. Can you think of another joint that bends this way?*

Answer on page 24

Moving your bones

Muscles are joined to bones. They make bones move by pulling them up and down. You can make string muscles for your model arm.

Tape here.

Cut two pieces of thick string the same length. Tape a piece to each side of your model arm, like this.

Tape this piece higher up.

Pull one string, then the other. Can you make the model move?

Muscles pull on bones. They cannot push, so they have to work in pairs. One muscle pulls in each direction, like the strings on your model.

Top muscle pulls to bend arm.

Bottom muscle pulls to straighten arm.

Muscles change shape to pull on bones. They bunch up and become shorter.

Broken bones

If you break a bone, your body can mend it. You have to wear a plaster cast so the broken ends line up properly.

Bend your arm. You can feel the muscle on top bunch up and go stiff. Then stretch your arm out hard. Feel how stiff the muscle underneath becomes.

Clench your fist.

15

Feeding your body

Everything you eat goes into your stomach and through some very long tubes inside you. Along the way, your body changes the food so it is easy to use.

Stomach

These tubes are called intestines.

Biting and chewing

Take a bite out of an apple. Which teeth do you bite it with? Now chew the piece you have bitten off. Do you chew it with the same teeth?

Look at your mouth in a mirror. Are your front teeth the same shape as the back ones?

Your front teeth are sharp-edged, for cutting through food.

Back teeth are big and lumpy, for grinding food into tiny pieces.

One gulp

Snakes cannot chew. They swallow their food whole, so it takes a long time to break down. A boa constrictor can take nine days to finish with a big meal. You take three days at most.

Chewing grinds food into small pieces and mixes it with your spit, or saliva. This makes the food easy to swallow.

Breaking down

There are chemicals in your saliva and in your stomach to break down food. They are called enzymes. Try this to see what enzymes can do.

Ask an adult to make a jelly.* When it is cool, but not set, divide it in half. Put pieces of kiwi fruit in one half. Leave both halves in a cool place.

Look at the jellies after a few hours. Have they both set?

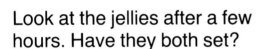

There is an enzyme in kiwi fruit that breaks down jelly. This stops it from setting.

*Also called gelatin (US).

Groans and gurgles

Sometimes your stomach rumbles after a meal. What you hear is the noise of food and air going along the tubes inside you.

Enzymes break down the food in your stomach into very tiny pieces, so they make a sort of soup.

Your blood takes these tiny pieces of food from your intestines to other parts of your body. You get rid of what you don't need when you go to the toilet.

Pumping blood

If you put your ear to a friend's chest, you can hear thumping. It is his heart beating. Each time it beats it fills with blood and squeezes it out again. The blood moves inside tubes called blood vessels.

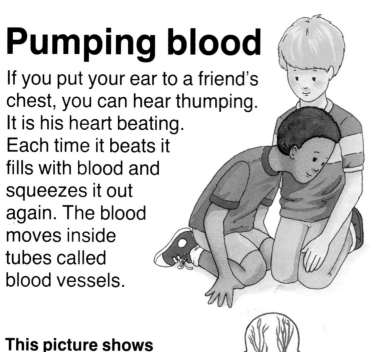

This picture shows where your heart and blood vessels are inside you.

Networks of blood vessels take blood to your lungs.

Your heart is slightly on the left side of your body.

Your blood vessels reach all over your body.

What blood carries

Your blood carries oxygen from the air you breathe. It takes the oxygen to your muscles, along with tiny pieces of food. The muscles use the oxygen and food to make energy.

Pumping hard

Your heart pumps your blood very strongly. You can even feel the beating in your arm.

Hold two fingers on your wrist, like this. Can you feel a regular throbbing?

Your fingers are over a blood vessel near the surface. You can feel the blood moving through the blood vessel. This beating is called your pulse.

Fast and slow

Flatten a small ball of clay and stick a toothpick in the middle.

Relax your arm and rest your hand on a table. Balance the clay on your wrist, where you can feel your pulse. Can you see the toothpick move?

Walk quickly for a while. Balance the clay on your wrist again. Now how many times does the toothpick move in 30 seconds?

You need a watch that shows seconds.

Squeezing hard

Your heart is about the size of your fist. Try this to see how strong it is.

Squeeze a tennis ball in one hand. Can you squash it?

Each time your heart beats, it squeezes as hard as you need to squeeze to squash the ball.

Walk quickly for a while. Balance the playdough on your wrist again. Now how many times does the toothpick move in 30 seconds?

When you exercise, your heart beats faster to send the blood around more quickly. Your muscles need more food and oxygen to make energy because they are using it up faster.

19

In control

Your brain is inside your head. It tells every part of your body what to do, even when you are asleep.

A bony case called your skull protects your brain.

Dreaming

Dreams can be strange, but scientists think they are your brain's way of making sense of things – either things that happened during the day, or even things you hear or feel in your sleep.

Reaction timer

When you catch something, your brain sends a message to your hand, telling it to catch. The faster the message travels, the faster you move, or react. You can test your reactions.

Cut a long thin piece of stiff cardboard. Draw lines across it and mark the top. This is your reaction timer.

Hold up the timer. Ask a friend to hold his hand near the bottom without quite touching it. Ask him to catch it when you drop it.

Write his name on the mark where he catches it. Then ask him to drop the timer for you.

The nearer the bottom you catch the timer, the faster your reactions are.

Automatic reactions

Your brain can make your body do lots of things without you even thinking about them. These automatic reactions are called reflexes. Ask a friend to help you make a reflex work.

Make a room dim by closing the curtains, then look at yourself in a mirror. Look at the middle of your eyes. The black parts in the middle are called your pupils.

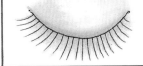

Pupil

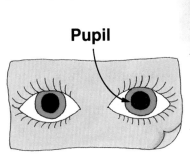

Can you see how big your pupils are? They get bigger in the dark to let in more light. This helps you to see better.

Blinking

You blink automatically. Every time you blink, water washes your eyes. It wipes away dust and other things that might hurt your eyes.

Now ask a friend to turn on the light. Watch your eyes very carefully in the mirror. What happens to your pupils?

Your pupils shrink automatically when the light gets stronger. Your brain makes them close up to keep too much light from getting into your eyes, because it could harm them.

Notes for parents and teachers

These notes will help answer questions that arise from the activities on earlier pages.

About your body (pages 2-3)

Your fingerprints are different from other people's because of a special code in every cell in your body, made of a chemical called DNA. This code tells your body how to grow – for example, whether you have blue eyes, and how tall you will be. It is a very complicated code and everyone's is different, except for identical twins, who may have the same fingerprints.

Touch (pages 4-5)

The ends of nerves in your skin, called receptors, send messages to your brain about what they feel. Some nerve endings detect pressure, some heat, cold, or pain. How sensitive any area of your skin is depends on how close together the nerve endings are. They are closest together in your fingertips and parts of your face, like your lips. This is why they are the most sensitive parts of your body.

Looking out (pages 6-7)

Light reflected off things goes into your eye through a hole called the pupil. Nerves inside your eye detect the light as it hits the back of your eye, and send a message to your brain about it. The brain interprets the pattern of the light as an image.

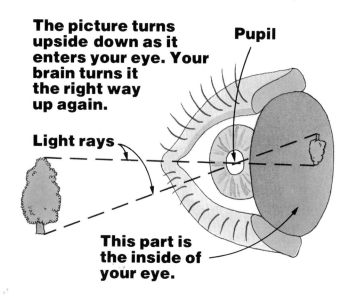

The picture turns upside down as it enters your eye. Your brain turns it the right way up again.

Pupil

Light rays

This part is the inside of your eye.

Speaking out (pages 8-9)

As the vocal cords are stretched and relaxed by the muscles around them, their edges become thinner and thicker. Thinner edges make a higher noise. Thicker ones make lower notes. Men have thicker, longer vocal cords than women. This is why they tend to have deeper voices.

Breathing (pages 12-13)

Air is a mixture of gases, one of which is called oxygen. It is the only part of air that your body uses. Oxygen from the air passes into your blood through the walls of your lungs. Your blood takes it to your muscles. They use it to make energy, producing a waste gas called carbon dioxide. Your blood takes the carbon dioxide back to your lungs and you breathe it out.

Pumping blood (pages 18-19)

You have big blood vessels close to your heart, which branch off into smaller and smaller vessels, to reach every part of your body. Blood travels away from your heart in blood vessels called arteries, and back to your heart in veins.

Your heart is a very strong muscle. Like all your other muscles, it needs blood to bring it oxygen and food, and exercise to keep fit.

Bones and muscles (pages 14-15)

Wrist joint

Spine

Ball and socket joint

There are lots of different types of joints between your bones. Your knees and elbows are like hinges. Your hips and shoulders are made like a ball in a socket, so they can turn in a circle. Your wrists have lots of small sliding bones in them to help them move to different positions easily. The joints in your spine enable it to curve but not bend at a sharp angle.

In control (pages 20-21)

Different parts of your brain do different jobs. One part works all the time to make sure you keep breathing. It also regulates your heartbeat. Other parts control speech and movement, thinking and memory. This shows you the jobs some parts of the brain do.

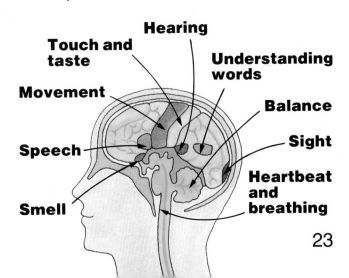

Hearing

Touch and taste

Understanding words

Movement

Balance

Speech

Sight

Heartbeat and breathing

Smell

Index

Answer to puzzle on page 14

Another joint that bends like your elbow is your knee.

First published in 1992 by Usborne Publishing Ltd, Usborne House, 83-85 Saffron Hill, London, EC1N 8RT, England. Copyright © 1992 Usborne Publishing Ltd.

Printed in Belgium. First published in America March 1993